Charlton Athletic Celebrity Fans

David C Ramzan

ALOBTH

Cover – left to right
Steve Rider, Sue Perkins,
Frankie Howerd, Billy Cotton and
Cheryl Baker

CONTENTS

Introduction

When I first began attending Charlton home games back in the mid-60s, the signature tune played as the teams came down the tunnel of the old distinctively designed West Stand was the well-established sound of Billy Cotton and his band's rendition, *When the Red, Red Robin (Comes Bob, Bob, Bobbin' Along)*. Perhaps not a melody to get the fans rocking in the isles, or rather on the terraces, leading up to the kick-off, but the song had been played out over the tannoy since the days when Charlton Athletic were a leading force in the First Division of the Football League, the equivalent of the Premier League for those too young to remember.

The song became part of the club's long illustrious heritage, and woe betide anyone suggesting, or attempting, to change the club's theme song, endeavouring to do away with it altogether, or even worse replacing it with a rock number!!

When specially recorded for the club by Billy Cotton and his band, Charlton were under the ownership of the wealthy Gliksten Brothers, Albert and Stanley, timber merchants from East London, who were well acquainted with show business impresarios of the entertainments world the Grade family, agents of Billy Cotton.

It was through the iconic rendition of *Red, Red Robin* that I first became aware of an association between the club and a star celebrity, as the Billy Cotton Band were then broadcasting on the BBC Radio Light Programme Sunday lunchtimes, as well as appearing on BBC Television Saturday evenings. Both programmes were broadcast up until 1968, the favourite radio listening and television viewing in the family household at the time, and when Billy Cotton and his band played the club's song, a few of us attempted to sing along with the chorus.

Charlton's old First Division rivals such as Chelsea, Manchester United, Arsenal, Liverpool, and Tottenham could claim a host of famous celebrity fans over the years, usually popping out of the woodwork when 'their' clubs were doing well, playing in a cup final or heading for the First Division league title. The Addicks however, have also had a fair share of celebrity fans who have declared their allegiance to the club at some point during their lives, before, during, or after becoming famous, the difference was, Charlton weren't well known for winning cups and titles.

Not only did stars of the entertainment world and silver screen come to watch Charlton's matches at The Valley, standing alongside fans on the terraces to cheer the team on, or in many cases, more likely, sitting in the West Stand seats, the club and its players have featured, and been mentioned, in several films and television productions over the years.

In this book, Star Addicks, I have included a selected number of celebrity fans, as well as a few who have had an interesting connection to the club, along with some noteworthy appearances by players in dramatised and fictional movies, television, and radio productions, and, on occasion, when the club and ground have featured in a film or television programme storyline.

Charlton matches and players have been created as cartoons and caricatures ever since the early 1900s, not too long after the club was formed, appearing in local and national papers when sports photography was in its infancy and photographs of players and matches, to accompany match and club reports, were few and far between, and the celebrities featured in Star Addicks are also represented as line drawn caricatures, reminiscent of football's good old days.

Syd Jorden's caricatures of the Charlton team, late-1920s

The limited number of footballing photographs available for reproduction in the press would usually feature clubs from the top division of the Football League, and very rarely would readers see an image of any match action or players from the lower leagues, unless they were involved in an exceptionally long cup run. As for non-league Charlton Athletic, although there are existing photographs from the days when the club was formed, none were produced in newsprint, and it would be a cartoon to first feature Charlton in a local newspaper published during November 1908, along with a report of the previous week's home match against the Royal Army Medical Corps, Charlton winning 8-0.

Many of these early cartoons refer to the club's connection to a fish, the haddock, associated with Arthur Bryan, a local fishmonger and supporter and patron of the club. Bryan handed out fish and chips to the players after a match, and paraded around a haddock nailed to a pole at games, to promote his business.

It was from this fish that Charlton Athletic acquired its unique nickname, The Addicks,

Charlton's Board late-1930s
Stanley Gliksten, Albert Gliksten, Robert Law,
David Clark, Dr John Montgomery

from how southeast Londoners pronounced the word haddock. Many of these early drawings have been reproduced in the book, *The Addicks Cartoons*, by Charlton fan Richard Redden.

As The Addicks rose up through the district leagues like a fish leaping up a succession of waterfalls, the club then winning promotion into the Football League, local and national newspapers began to include line drawing player caricatures and comic strip style stories, usually depicted in a comical manner, the main match action. A series of footballer caricatures were also used to promote the buying of cigarettes, various brands including a cigarette card with a caricature of a famous player of the day in each pack, which included members of the Charlton team.

ARTHUR TURNER   CHRIS DUFFY   HAROLD PHIPPS

Kicking off in the world of entertainment

After Charlton won promotion from the Second Division under the direction of manager Jimmy Seed at the end of the 1935-1936 season, finishing in second place behind Manchester United, First Division football returned to southeast London for the first time since one-time near neighbours Arsenal relocated to North London in 1913.

Although missing out on winning the 1936-1937 First Division title by just four points, two wins back in the day, Manchester City lifting the league trophy, Charlton had certainly made a remarkable start to their first season in the top tier of the English Football League. The rise through three divisions in successive seasons brought the club plenty of fame and notoriety, not only at home but also abroad. Towards the end of their promotion-winning season, Charlton were invited to tour overseas, in Spain, and North and South Africa, and the following season offers came in to tour Argentina, Czechoslovakia, France, Romania, Russia, and South Africa.

However, on a business trip to North America, club owner and chairman, Albert Gliksten, arranged for Charlton to tour the United States and Canada during the close season, possibly as this would be the most lucrative to take part in as the club were on course to make a loss at the end of the financial year. Previously, Charlton stepped up as a late replacement for a match against the French International team after Italy had pulled out, Charlton beating the French in Paris 5-2. Charlton's footballing exploits brought plenty of media attention, in the broadsheets at home and abroad, as well as on the silver screen in news reports shown between feature films at picture houses.

Pathé News had already been along to The Valley to film the manager and players during a training session, and the club would feature again on film during the Second World War, when playing in two successive War Cup Finals, losing one and winning another, and then in the 1946 FA Cup Final, losing to Derby 4-1, and the following year beating Burnley 1-0 to lift the FA Cup for the first time, all captured on film.

It would not be too long however until Charlton's players themselves were appearing in feature films alongside stars of the silver screen.

At the beginning of the 1950s, several professional and

amateur footballers were drafted in as extras, playing in match sequences for the British-made film, *Small Town Story*,

Yesteryear Extras!!!

starring Susan Shaw Donald Houston, Alan Wheatly, and Kent Walton in his first and only screen role.

Although a young Kent Walton began his entertainment career as an actor, he also commentated on football and tennis, and would go on to become well known as the voice of wrestling, for ITV's, *World of Sport*, the wrestling matches taking place on Saturday afternoons before the full-time football results service.

Set in the world of Association Football, *Small Town Story* featured several football legends including Denis Compton and Charlton's own 1947 FA Cup winner and defender Peter Croker. However, unlike Compton who had a speaking part, Croker's performance was entirely on the pitch. Leading up to when the film was released in 1953, Croker had come to the end of his time at Charlton and was turning out for Harvey's Sports football team.

Released principally as a dramatic thriller, Walton, playing the role of a talented footballer, Canadian former serviceman named Bob Regan, is lured away from the lower division Oldchester United by a femme fatale who persuades him to sign up for Arsenal.

The story revolves around the sleazy world of financial football corruption, purely fiction of course, Walton, or rather Regan, then reflects on the error of his ways and re-joins Oldchester, where his goal-scoring prowess is fundamental in the club's promotion, Croker, unnamed in the credits, playing in some neatly staged football match action sequences.

Two years after the release of *Small Town Story*, comedian and actor Arthur Askey starred in a black and white

Full steam ahead playmates!!!

comedy, *The Love Match*, where all of Charlton's players appeared alongside Askey, and co-stars Glen Melvyn, William Franklyn, Thora Herd, 'Bond Girl' Shirley Eaton and

James Kenny, who played Askey's footballer son, Percy Brown.

In the production, based on a stage play written by Glen Melvyn, Askey portrays Lancastrian football-loving steam train engine driver, Bill Brown, whose goal in life is to finish his shift to get to the match on time to watch his team, 'City', play.

Bill's son Kenny, however, is on the books of local rivals 'United', players of both fictional teams represented by Charlton players for filming in close-up action, with the match action sequences utilising footage from games played at The Valley, Bolton's Burnden Park, and Cardiff City.

At the beginning of the film 'United' are beating 'City', where Askey and his coal stoker Melvyn then drive the

Men of the match!!!

steam train at top speed to finish their shift in time to get to the match before full time, arriving outside The Valley on motorbike and sidecar. During the game, Charlton's Eddie Firmani was filmed in close-up scoring a penalty.

After the release of The Love Match in February 1955, Firmani was in his final season at Charlton and was sold to Italian club Sampdoria for an English Football League record transfer fee of £35,000, plus £5,000 signing on fee, a car, and a flat in Genoa, not too bad back in the day. In Firmani's own words, he was now playing, 'football with the millionaires', the line he used as the title of his autobiography. Scoring twenty-six goals in his final season at Charlton, Firmani was sorely missed, and at the end of the 1956-1957 season, legendary manager, Jimmy Seed had been sacked and the club, finishing at the foot of the Division One table, were relegated.

At the beginning of the 1963-1964 season, Second Division Charlton re-sign Firmani from Italian club Genoa, attendances were on the rise, and Charlton just miss out on bringing First Division football back to The Valley after finishing in fourth place. With The Valley averaging crowds of just over 18,000, a film production company were back at the club to shoot scenes for the film The Silent Playground, a British thriller written and directed by Stanley Goulder, a documentary maker whose style gives the movie, shot on location around Charlton and Woolwich, a gritty realism.

The story centres around barbiturates handed out to children waiting in a cinema queue and at a local playground, the youngsters, believing they are sweets eat them and are taken ill. The hunt is then on to find the culprit. Leading up

We were Winning 1-0!!!

to the movie's climax, where several scenes were filmed at
The Valley, inside and outside the ground, along with match
sequences and views of the crowd. In one scene, filmed at
Floyd Road, the mother of three missing children arrives
with the police to pick up her boyfriend, a Charlton
supporter, to help in the search. Eventually, all ends well,
the children are found alive, although suffering the effects
from eating the medication, and the guilty party handing out
the drugs, a mental patient, is apprehended.

During the early-1970s, Charlton were relegated to the
Third Division for the first time in the club's history. After
three seasons playing in the third tier of the Football League,
Charlton win promotion and are back on the small screen
in the situation television comedy series, *Lucky Feller*,
starring Peter Armitage, Cheryl Hall, and a young David
Jason. Written by talented author and playwright, Terence

Frisby, born in New Cross, Armitage and Jason play riveling plumbing brothers living in Brockley. During the run of thirteen episodes, it's alluded to that Randolph 'Randy' Mepstead, played by Armitage, is a Millwall supporter, while his brother Bernard 'Shorty' Mepstead, Jason, supports Charlton, their love interests in the series, Kath Peake, played by Cheryl Hall.

Jason's character, 'Shorty', is in love with Kath, his brother 'Randy's' girlfriend, the stories revolve around this love triangle, where both 'Randy' and Kath, take advantage of 'Shorty's' naivety and good nature.

There were few references to both clubs during the series run, however, scarfs hanging prominently in each of the brother's bedrooms, show a flash of red and white of Charlton, and blue and white of Millwall. At the time of filming, the Lions, or Spanners as Charlton fans refer to our near neighbours, were  playing at the old The Den, down in the Third Division.

David Jason would go on to appear in another, more successful long-running situation comedy, Charlton once again playing an important part in an episode of *Only Fools and Horses*, and both Jason and Charlton would later feature in a made-for-TV movie, but more of these later. Around the time of *Lucky Feller*, ITV were broadcasting a three-part series, *Saturday's Heroes*, showcasing stories of football and footballers, one of which, *Ha'way the Lads*, featured Charlton's greatest manager, Jimmy Seed. The title, *Ha'way the Lads*, is taken from a term used by miners, of which Seed was one before making a career in football.

Produced by Thames Television and directed by Canadian filmmaker Frank Cvitanovich, a former American footballer, the drama documentary charted Seed's early life, from schoolboy to professional footballer, his determination to

Ha'way Jimmy!!!

get away from a life working down the mines of County Durham, and how he overcame two gas attacks during the First World War, resulting in rejection by his boyhood club, Sunderland FC, because of his health issues.

Seed, superbly portrayed by John Bowler in his first television performance, is told, at the age of twenty-three, his footballing career is over as the inhalation of mustard gas during the war has damaged his lungs, and it's back down the mines for him.

Unexpectedly, Seed's football career is rescued when invited to join Mid Rhonda FC, and while Seed is shown travelling by train on his way to Wales, his future football achievements as a player and then a manager are revealed as the documentary comes to an end.

For those younger Charlton fans who are unaware of Jimmy Seed's career, after leaving Mid Rhonda Seed signed for Tottenham Hotspur, winning promotion from the Second Division and then winning the FA Cup, and during Seed's time with Spurs, he was called up to play for England. After transferring to Sheffield Wednesday, Seed was made captain and the club went on to win two successive First Division championship titles.

Retiring from playing, Seed first managed Clapton Orient, now Leyton Orient, before joining Charlton Athletic in 1933, where he guided the club from Third Division to First Division in successive seasons, took the club to four cup final appearances at Wembley, winning the War Cup in 1944, and the FA Cup in 1947.

Sixteen months after the broadcast of *Ha'way the Lads*, Charlton featured in a BBC television play, *The Back Page*, based around when Notts County visited The Valley for a Second Division fixture on 29 January 1977, the play taking place mostly in the press box, intercut with scenes from the actual match.

The story centres around a young sports reporter, a Notts County fan, and the mockery he encounters from the older seasoned newspaper hacks. Written by Andrew

Nickolds and Stan Hey, the latter would go on to write a large proportion of *The Manageress* television series, the sports reporters in the press box were played by Roger Avon, Henry Moxon, John Salthouse, Graham Stark, and Howard Southern.

The half-hour play was one of a British drama anthology series, *Second City Firsts* broadcast over nine seasons. In the play, John Salthouse's character, going by the nickname of 'Binoculars', has travelled down to Charlton from Nottingham to cover the match for his local paper, the young reporter jumping for joy when Notts County

unexpectedly take the lead in the twenty-seventh minute. The situation soon changes, however, when Charlton are awarded a penalty in the oddest of circumstances. When Charlton's Phil Warman appeals for a penalty, referee Tony

Glasson waves play on, however, Notts County's Dave Smith thinks he hears a whistle and picks up the ball in his own area, the referee having no alternative than to award a penalty. Charlton's Bob Curtis scores from the spot just before halftime, and the match eventually finishes in a 1 – 1 draw.

At the end of that season which featured in the play, Charlton finished in seventh position of the Second Division, one place above their opponents Notts County on goal difference.

Over the following ten years, there was very little improvement for The Addicks on the pitch, and very few appearances on screen, apart from occasional game day highlights on *Match of the Day* and *The Big Match*. Charlton were relegated at the end of the 1979-1980 season, but only played a season in the Third Division, winning promotion under the guidance of manager and former player Mike Bailey. By this time attendance had dropped to around 6,000 die-hard fans, then the club were back on television news reports for all the wrong reasons, after almost going into administration and surviving going bust, Charlton are forced to leave The Valley and relocate to Selhurst Park, for financial reason, or so the owners alleged.

During the wilderness years Charlton unbelievably won promotion to the First Division, where there was plenty of televised football coverage, but nothing in the dramatic sphere of film and television until mentioned in an episode of the long-running television comedy series *Only Fools and Horses*. First airing in September 1981, *Only Fools and Horses* ran for seven series and several specials, up until 2003.

Written by Balham-born John Sullivan, the series' main stars were David Jason as Derek 'Del Boy' Trotter, Nicholas Lyndhurst as Rodney Trotter Del Boy's younger brother, Lennard Pearce as Grandad, and Buster Merryfield as Uncle Albert. Later in the series along came Rodney's love interest, Cassandra, played by Gwyneth Strong, her character behind the revealment of her future husband's connection to The Addicks.

In episode 46 of series 6, *Little Problems*, broadcast on 5 February 1989, Rodney and Cassandra are at the alter on their wedding day ready to take their vows, the vicar then utters these immortal words, " ….I call upon these persons here present, to witness that I, Rodney Charlton Trotter….". The congregation in fits of laughter are astounded to hear Rodney's middle name for the first time, along with almost nineteen-million UK viewers. Later in the episode, at Rodney and Cassandra's reception, Marlene tells Del-Boy she didn't know Rodney's middle name was

Charlton, Del-Boy explains their mother was a fan, Marlene asks "What, Charlton Heston?", Del Boy replies "No, Charlton Athletic".

This episode resulted in Charlton fans later adopting Rodney Charlton Trotter as one of their own, and the production of flags, beach towels, stickers, and posters adapted from the *Only Fools and Horses* motif, with the words Rodney Charlton Trotter emblazoned across the centre.

The year after this episode was broadcast, Charlton were relegated from the First Division, however, after a successful campaign by the fans, and under new owners, the club would soon be returning to a refurbished Valley.

After several seasons consolidating in the second tier of the Football League, Charlton were then promoted through the Play-Offs in 1998.

Although relegation followed after only a season in the Premiership, Charlton returned as Champions at the end of the 1999-2000 season and were back on television in Sky One's *Dream Team*, a British sports drama, broadcast over ten series between 1997 and 2007, the programme chronicled the on and off the field story of fictional Premier League club Harchester United. Footage from actual Premier League matches were used in the production, and several club managers and staff, including Charlton's Alan Curbishley, made cameo appearances in the storylines.

Actors also played the parts of footballers in Charlton's squad, in one episode Curbishley is filmed on The Valley pitch introducing two new signings to the media, the characters Rose and Christie. Curbishley is also often seen addressing the Charlton players in the team dressing room before playing fictional matches, and in one scene when Charlton are up against Harchester, Charlton's Clive Mendonca brings down an opposition player in the Charlton penalty area, the referee waving play on, and then, when

Mendonca is brought down in the Harchester area, a penalty is then awarded against them. In the storyline Charlton win 3-0, with goals scored by John Robinson, Neil Redfearn, and the penalty from Mendonca....but now back to reality.

When Curbishley left Charlton at the end of the 2005-2006 season, not to go into acting, Charlton's Premier League dream was also over, as the club soon suffered relegation under a succession of three managers in one season, unbelievable even if in a storyline of a fictional football show.

The misery of Charlton's long-time suffering fans was reflected at the time in a line from the 2006 psychological thriller, *Notes on a Scandal*, a complex story of the relationship between two female teachers, starring Dame Judi Dench and Cate Blanchett. In one scene, Dame Judi, playing a spinster veteran teacher, during a heated and

impassioned discussion with her colleague remarks, quite bluntly, "My father was a supporter of Charlton Athletic. Never seemed to give him any pleasure."

Charlton supporters suffered further indignation when the club plummeted down into the third tier of the Football League after relegated at the end of the 2008-2009 season.

While languishing in the First Division, the old Third Division, Charlton were featured in a one-off television drama, *Albert's Memorial*, broadcast in September 2010, following the story of three Second World War veterans, David Jason as Harry, David Warner as Frank and Michael Jayston as Albert. On his deathbed, Albert's dying wish is to be buried on a hillside near Hindenburg, Germany, where the three comrades encountered Russian allied troops taking up position in the final stages of the war. When Albert dies, his family refuses to grant his final wish, so Harry and Frank kidnap Albert's body, and drive off in

Harry's black cab on a series of adventures to Hindenburg, with Albert strapped to the roof in a coffin.

Harry, a Charlton fan, while staying overnight in a motel, attempts to get Sky on the television, so he can watch the Charlton match, much to the annoyance of Frank, and then, after the coffin with Albert inside falls from the cab, the coffin too badly damaged to use for a burial, on arrival at

the hillside, Albert is laid to rest wrapped in Harry's Charlton flag, even though Albert was never a fan.

In another time and another place, Doctor Who writer, Chris Chibnall, penned the script for the 2011 television drama United, based on Manchester United's 'Busby Babes' and the 1958 Munich air crash, particularly the aftermath and the role assistant manager Jimmy Murphy played in the club's resurgence while Matt Busby was recuperating. The role of Murphy was portrayed by David Tennent, who had previously played the tenth Doctor, in the world-wide well-known BBC science fiction series *Doctor Who*, in which the companion of the Seventh Doctor's incarnation, Ace, supported Charlton.

At the beginning of *United*, young Bobby Charlton, played by Jack O'Connell, makes his debut for Manchester United up against Charlton Athletic at Old Trafford in October 1956. Running out onto the pitch, the Charlton players,

Didn't one of my companions support the Addicks?

full of confidence and believing they are a better team, are heard making disparaging comments about United's youngsters, then, coming off the pitch at the end of the match, the Charlton players can't believe they have been vastly outplayed by 'Busby's Babes', losing the fixture 4-2, Bobby Charlton scoring a brace.

In reality, The Addicks had been on a poor run of results where up to the match against United had lost eight of their first eleven fixtures, winning two and drawing one. The season ended in relegation for Charlton, while Manchester United finished top of the First Division, and would be flying off to European competition the following season, a journey which ended in disaster.

Not only have Charlton featured in the world of show business, in dramatised film and television productions, but stars of rock music have also performed at The Valley too. On 18 May 1974, The Who were top of the bill in a concert supported by acts Montrose, Lindisfarne, Bad Company, Lou Reed, Humble Pie, and Maggie Bell.

The Who, one of the most exhilarating loudest live bands of the time, chose The Valley because, according to Pete Townsend, it had particular acoustic qualities and excellent views of the stage from the terraces. The concert was a raucous affair, with around 50,000 concertgoers packed

into The Valley and there were plenty of scuffles on the pitch area, much like a match day back then. On one occasion Lindisfarne band members also began throwing beer over a policeman who was attempting to gain access to the stage.

...and one day I'll be manager here!!!

GET YOUR WHO T-SHIRTS HERE!

THE WHO AT THE VALLEY

At the time of the concert, The Who were then managed by Bill Curbishley, whose younger brother Alan would one day play for Charlton. During the concert, young Curbishley was given the task of going around the crowd selling T-Shirts. Two years later The Who were back at The Valley, where, with the help of some 75,000 screaming fans, the rock band broke the record books for the loudest concert of all time at 126 decibels, a record which continues to stand today, as the Guinness Book of Records scrapped this particular listed record due to the damage loud music can cause to peoples hearing.

After Charlton's return to The Valley, the club applied for permission to hold future concerts but were initially turned down by the council. When all sides of The Valley were rebuilt, apart from the South Stand away end, later named The Jimmy Seed Stand, the club were eventually granted a licence to hold the first open-air concert since The Who, with the star turn Rocket Man himself, Watford supporter Elton John, performing in the summer of 2006.

The season after the concert, The Addicks were up against Elton's club Watford, recently promoted to the Premier League, however, Charlton and Watford fell back down to earth with a bump, as both clubs were relegated at the season's end.

Charlton have also been featured in various factual and historical publications over the years, including manager and player biographies, such as *The Jimmy Seed Story*, *The Sam Bartram Autobiography,* and Garry Nelson's *Left Foot Forward*, alongside various statistical books, annuals, magazines, and club histories, and a range of novels, Paul Breen's *The Charlton Men* and *The Bones of a Season*, and David Lodge's *Out of the Shelter*.

Dotun Adebayo

Beginning alphabetically, Dotun Adebayo may not be one of Charlton's most well know celebrity fans, but the Nigerian-born radio presenter, writer, and publisher often mentions supporting The Addicks during his radio programmes and on his Twitter account.

Presenter of BBC Radio 5 Live's *World Football Phone In*, an early morning radio programme broadcast between 2.00 am and 4.00 am, part of *Up All Night*, Adebayo discusses the global game with football pundits including Tim Vicary, Mark

Gleeson, and Paul Saras, along with football fans, occasionally Charlton supporters, calling into the show.

Passionate about the game of football and its positive effects it can have on people from all parts of the world, Adebayo came to Britain to join his parents when he was only six years old, and although growing up in north London, rather than follow the Spurs or the Gooners, he surprisingly decided on The Addicks. However, the radio presenter concedes, travelling across the river to southeast London can often be a nightmare journey.

When England were looking for a new manager after Fabio Capello resigned due to a dispute with The Football Association, it was Adebayo who championed Chris Powell for the position before Charlton were sold to Roland Duchâtelet and things went rapidly downhill.

Before beginning a career in broadcasting, the young Adebayo had thoughts of becoming an actor, and was cast alongside veteran actor Vincent Price, making a brief appearance in a Hammer House of Horror film, and later he had a part in the Bond film, *Diamonds Are forever*.

After joining the National Youth Theatre, Adebayo also appeared in several plays, then, while studying at University he presented two radio programmes for the student radio station, his introduction to radio broadcasting. In 2009, Adebayo was awarded an MBE, for services to the arts.

As an Addicks fan, Adebayo has admitted the worst aspect of watching Charlton is being 'done over' in the last minute, something which a majority of Charlton fans can all relate to.

It's the 22nd century and Charlton win the Champions League!!!

Sophie Aldred

Greenwich-born Sophie Aldred grew up in Blackheath, attending Blackheath High School and singing in the choir of St James' Kidbrooke. A Charlton supporter from a young age, Aldred continued following The Addicks after enrolling as a drama student at the University of Manchester.

Working in children's theatre after graduating, while appearing in the chorus of the musical *Fiddler on the Roof*, Aldred was cast as the character Ace in the BBC television series *Doctor Who* in 1987. Throughout the run of nine stories, Aldred played a sixteen-year-old human companion to Sylvester McCoy's Doctor, her character described as 'a fighter, not a screamer', the pair bringing the original *Doctor Who* series to a conclusion in 1989.

In several episodes, Ace, whose name in the series was Dorothy, was often seen wearing a black bomber jacket with the word 'Ace' in large red letters emblazoned across the back, the front and sleeves covered in an assortment of patches and badges, one of which was Charlton's distinctive club badge, the version which had the white roundel, red centre, and gold sword motif.

Although Aldred's character was supposedly from Perivale in West London, north of the River Thames, Ace is obviously an Addicks fan, mentioning Charlton had picked up three points when looking for the club's results in the Daily Mirror.

Since bowing out at the end of the original *Doctor Who* series, Aldred, considered by many fans to be one of the Doctor's most popular companions, has appeared in various children's and educational television programmes and theatre productions, later reprising her role as Ace in Big Finish *Doctor Who* audio plays and television specials. Ace returned for the BBC's Doctor Who Centenary episode, *The Power of the Doctor*, and wore her original black bomber jacket, with the Charlton badge.

Gemma Arterton

Who would have believed The Addicks would have a Bond girl as a fan? When Gemma Arterton first came to matches at The Valley it was with her father, a Charlton supporter, Arterton suggesting to Lorraine Kelly, on her morning show *Lorraine*, it was probably because they were the cheapest club for him to take her to.

Born in Gravesend, Arterton attended Gravesend Grammar School for Girls, before leaving at the age of sixteen to study acting at Dartford's Miskin Theatre, North West Kent College. Before heading down the road for a career in theatre and film, Arterton worked on a beauty counter as a make-up sales girl, as well as a karaoke hostess in a pub near Waterloo, Honest Dave's Karaoke Bar, to earn money to pay her rent and bills. Honest Dave told Arterton, if things in the bar started getting too rowdy, sing the song from *Titanic*, Celine Dion's *My Heart Will Go On*, which seemed to calm the punters down.

Leaving shop and bar work behind, in 2007, Arterton made her professional theatrical debut at the Globe in Shakespeare's *Love's Labour's Lost*, and in the same year appeared in her first film, *St Trinian's*. Winning an Empire Award for Best Newcomer playing Strawberry Fields in the Bond film *Quantum of Solace*. During her appearance on *Lorraine*, to promote her latest film *Tamara Drew*, released in 2010, Arterton was overjoyed when presented with a Charlton shirt, no doubt a much better gift than when receiving the award for best newcomer.

At Charlton's First Division fixture against Southend United on 8 April 2017, more presentations took place at the end of a fundraising walk for the Charlton Upbeats, but it was Arterton's younger sister, Hannah, also an actor, who handed out medals to Charlton's Upbeats after playing Brighton & Hove Albion, the finale of the Upbeats fundraising walk.

Cheryl Baker

Eurovision Contest winner with the group Bucks Fizz in 1981, singer and television presenter Cheryl Baker could often be found at The Valley mixing with fans and players in the club's exclusive portacabin bar after Charlton's return to The Valley in 1992. Baker's infectious bubbly, happy-go-lucky personality was always a welcome distraction after a Charlton loss.

Although originating in Bethnal Green, Baker and her family moved south of the river, residing in Gravesend. In the same year the club returned home, Baker, then living in Eltham, married Hollies base player Steve Stroud in Lewisham.

During the late 1980s, Baker was a guest on Charlton's fledgling radio show, *Charlton Chat*, broadcast by Radio Thamesmead, the Bucks Fizz star helping out to promote the Back to The Valley Campaign and The Valley Party, Baker's support for Charlton generating plenty of media interest and much-needed publicity for The Addicks.

Continuing to perform with Mike Nolan and Jay Aston, under the title The Fizz, Baker has been known to occasionally rip off her skirt during a performance of the group's Eurovision Song Contest winner, *Making Your Mind Up*. Releasing several singles herself, when not recording and touring, Baker has appeared on various television shows as a presenter and special guest, as well as taking part in various reality productions, and theatrical performances.

Now living in Ightham Kent, Baker has thrown herself into supporting and raising funds for various charitable causes, taking part in, and completing, the London Marathon for the charity baker founded after former Bucks Fizz member Mike Nolan suffered a head injury in a road accident the group were involved in while on tour. Along with touring, recording, and charity work, this leaves now leaves little time for Baker to get along to watch her favourite club at, *The Land of Make Believe*, The Valley.

Valley Floyd Road the mist rolling in from the Thames...

UP THE ADDICKS

Dave Berry

Award-winning radio presenter Dave Berry, a regular attendee for Charlton fixtures at The Valley, was appointed youth services ambassador for the Charlton Community Trust in 2012.

Born in Lewisham, Berry's family lived in the Charlton area, however, the first game he was taken to was, in fact, Arsenal versus Wimbledon, during the time when Charlton were ground sharing at Selhurst Park.

After the club's return to The Valley, Berry and his mates were regulars in the North Stand for home games.

Now a successful journalist, and television and radio presenter, Berry began his working career at a vintage clothes shop in South London, The Observatory, before he then joined a model agency and then co-founded the tailoring brand October House, making bespoke suits for the famous. One of October's clients was Charlton's midfield maestro Scott Parker before he decided Charlton no longer suited him and then transferred to Chelsea.

When Charlton won through to the Play-Off final, Berry was running a club night at the Trafalgar Tavern, Greenwich, but managed to get to the final and back ready to present his show, even after extra time and penalties, undoubtedly there was plenty of partying at the riverside pub that night.

For Charlton's 25th Back to The Valley Anniversary, Berry was involved in another dramatic penalty shoot-out when he took on the role of manager for a team of Charlton Legends, with Steve Gritt as captain. The opponents on the day were another team of Addicks Legends, managed by Keith Peacock, with Alan Curbishley acting as his team's captain.

The match, which took place at The Valley to raise funds for the club's Community Trust in September 2017, finished in a dramatic 3-3 draw, however, Berry's side ended up the loses after the penalty shoot-out decider, in which Super Clive Mendonca scored from the spot.

Björn Borg

Five-times Wimbledon champion tennis ace Swedish-born Björn Borg spoke of his and his family's support of Charlton at the Royal Albert Hall in 2007, while promoting a tour of tennis champions

Borg became a fan through his grandfather, who first went to watch The Addicks when the team were touring Sweden during the late-1930s, at the time Charlton were one of the top teams in the First Division, and Borg's family home was stacked with club memorabilia and flags.

The Borg family's support for Charlton was further reinforced when Jimmy Seed signed Swedish International forward, Hans Jeppson, for the Addicks towards the end of the 1950-1951 season, when the team were struggling toward the bottom of the First Division table, the Swede scoring nine goals in eleven games, which kept Charlton clear of relegation.

It was said Jeppson was an excellent tennis player and would often play a few games against his friend, and Borg's father, Rune, who was a table-tennis champion himself. It was Rune, who, like his own father, followed Charlton, and took his own son, the future tennis Grand Slam World Champion, to watch The Addicks for the very first time.

Although the young Borg played football during the summer months, and ice hockey in the winter months, his chosen sport was tennis, a game which would take him all around the world competing in Grand Slams and international tournaments, and wherever he was, Borg has said he'd always check on the club's results.

Presented with a Charlton shirt during a trip to Britain, Borg added this to his collection of replica club shirts which had been sent to him as gifts, the former tennis star admitting he often wears an Addicks top when at home around the house.

Oi, oi charlton!!!

Garry Bushell

Newspaper columnist, music journalist, television presenter, and singer in the Cockney Oi bands, GBX, and the Gonads, Garry Bushell is a long-time Charlton supporter from Woolwich.

Bushell attended Charlton Manor Primary School, a short distance from The Valley, and then went to Colfe's Grammar School, but at the age of just four, before he began his schooling, Bushell was educated in the ways of supporting The Addicks when he was taken to The Valley for the first time by his mother and father.

It was while at secondary school when Bushell took his first steps into the world of entertainment, performing with Pink Tent, a group that evolved into the punk band the Gonads, formed in 1977, at a house on Indus Road Charlton. Bushell's band began playing their first live gigs at The Lads of the Village pub, adjacent to where The Addicks played their first-ever game on Siemens Meadow back in the early 1900s.

Although taken on as a Charlton apprentice player, at the age of eighteen, Bushell joined the International Socialists and then began writing for the Socialist Worker, swapping the game of football for the craft of journalism. Moving on to Fleet Street, writing for the *Sun*, *Evening Standard,* and *Daily Mirror*, although Bushell was well known for his controversial political and socialistic views and opinions, in 1999, the journalist was named critic of the year at the UK Press Awards, and then critic of the year in 2007 by the Heritage Foundation.

Residing in Sidcup, Bushell has been a season ticket holder for many years and often mentions Charlton on his own website, where, in one of his articles, *Campaign Corner – There Will Always Be An England*, he offers readers his own patriotic thoughts on what England means to him, which included Bubble and Squeak, Carry On Films, Aston Martins, and Charlton Athletic, the club listed in between Charlie Drake and Casuals.

I can see The Valley!!!

Charlie Clements

Winning several magazine and television soap awards playing the role of Bradley Banning in BBC's popular soap series *EastEnders*, Sidcup-born Charlie Clements has been a Charlton fan since a young boy, and when making an appearance on Sky's Saturday morning show Soccer AM in 2006, spoke fervently of his support of The Addicks.

Clements began acting at the age of four, and during his career has appeared in various stage, film, television, and documentary productions which included portraying the locally-born King of England, and keen footballer himself, Henry Tudor, in the production *The Six Queens of Henry VIII*.

While still in education, Clements learned to play rhythm guitar and is a member of the band Brooks Live.

In between his acting roles, playing in a band, and getting along to The Valley, Clements went back to acting school and graduated from RADA in 2014 with a masters.

During the Covid Pandemic, with theatres closed and television productions brought to a halt, and with very little chance of getting to The Valley to watch his team play, when games were postponed and then fixtures took place behind locked doors, like many other actors who were required to adapt their working situation to support themselves and their family, Clements switched from acting to take up another trade, cooking. When an opportunity to work at a local garden centre came along, Clements was employed as a chef, until placed on furlough.

Almost immediately after lockdown, Clements appeared in the world's longest-running theatrical production, Agatha Christie's famous murder mystery, *The Mousetrap*, which only closed due to Lockdown, cast as Detective Sergeant Trotter, assigned to report on the situation at Monkswell Manor.

When *The Mousetrap* was first performed on stage in 1952, Charlton had been performing in the top tier of the Football League for sixteen years, however, the curtain came down on The Addicks when their own long run in the First Division ended in tragedy when relegated in 1957.

Billy Cotton

Associated with Charlton through the club's signature tune, *The Red, Red Robin*, a version specially recorded by Billy Cotton and his band, Cotton was a friend of the Grade brothers, a family of theatrical entrepreneurs involved in the world of show business, who were themselves, friends of the Gliksten brothers, timber merchants and owners of The Addicks.

Cotton was often invited to Charlton's matches at The Valley and became a lifelong fan, although, in his younger years, he was an amateur player for Brentford and then Wimbledon. Scoring on his home debut for Brentford, in Cotton's second game, playing away at Millwall, he led the Lions on a merry song and dance, scoring twice!!

Born in Westminster, Cotton sang in a choir and began his musical career playing the drums before falsifying his age to join the army, serving with the Royal Fusiliers at the outbreak of the First World War. Posted to Malta and then Egypt, Cotton saw action during the Gallipoli campaign.

Earning a commission, at the age of just nineteen, Cotton learned to pilot Bristol Fighter aircraft, flying solo for the first time in 1918, on the same day the Royal Flying Core became the Royal Air Force.

After leaving the forces, Cotton had several jobs before forming his own dance band in 1924, then, during the Second World War, toured France to entertain the troops.

Seeking the thrill of speed, Cotton attempted, but just failed, to break the land speed world record, and competed as a racing driver at Brooklands, finishing fourth in the 1949, British Grand Prix.

In the same year, he raced in the Grand Prix, Cotton's band began performing for the BBC, in a Sunday lunchtime radio show, *The Billy Cotton Band Show*, which ran until 1968, the band also performed in televised shows for BBC TV. It was during his performances on radio and television when Cotton's agents were Lew and Leslie Grade.

Charlton Nil !!!

Jim Davidson

Stand-up comedian, Jim Davidson, came to public attention when appearing on ITV's *New Faces* talent show, however, Charlton fans of the 1970s, will remember Davidson learning his trade on the southeast London comedy circuit, often performing his 'Nick, Nick' routine in pubs down the Old Kent Road.

Davidson was born in Greenwich and grew up living in Kidbrooke, a few miles from The Valley, where he would go to watch Charlton with his schoolmates. Although a very vocal Charlton fan, Davidson became a director of AFC Bournemouth in the 1980s, his performances on and off stage, and the comedian's risqué jokes and bawdy acts, have caused much controversy. On occasion, Davidson has even upset his fellow Addicks supporters, specifically when referring to the club as 'Charlton Nil', although, at the time, Charlton weren't probably scoring many goals?

After attending St Austin's School Charlton, Davidson played drums in a pub band and was employed as a supermarket shelf stacker, a travel agency clerk, a Walls ice cream cashier, and a reprographics operative, before accidentally finding his destined career as an entertainer. When a comedian failed to turn up for a spot in a Woolwich pub, where Davidson and his mates were drinking, urged on by his companions, up he stepped and took the comedian's place.

A supporter of the armed forces and various other charities, Davidson launched the British Forces Foundation in 1999, and was awarded an OBE for his services to charity.

Often seen at The Valley, in the members' bar enjoying a few beers before and after games, along with hosting Charlton events, Davidson occasionally takes a detour around the streets of Woolwich and Kidbrooke, to the places where he grew up. Davidson launched his own YouTube channel, sharing his views on news stories and topical subjects of the day, including all woes that come with being a Charlton fan.

Chris Difford and Glenn Tilbrook

When Charlton reached the Championship Play-Off final at Wembley in 1998, members of the band Squeeze, Chris Difford and Glen Tilbrook, wrote and recorded a double-sided single *Down in The Valley*, released on the independent label Quixotic Records, a tribute to their local club.

Difford, born in Greenwich, and Tilbrook, born in Woolwich, first met after guitarist and vocalist Tilbrook, placed an ad in a local shop looking for another guitarist to join him, and Difford was the only one to answer. Tilbrook then brought in a school friend, keyboard player Jools Holland, and a fourth member, drummer Paul Gunn, to form a group, which, after going under several names, became the New Wave band Squeeze. Taking the name of Velvet Underground's album *Squeeze*, released in 1973, the band first began performing around the local music scene of Greenwich and Deptford.

Their debut EP, *Packet of Three*, was released in 1977, on the Deptford Fun Label, this was followed by their first two highest hit singles to date, *Take Me I'm Yours* and *Bang Bang*, which Squeeze produced themselves. On a majority of the band's releases, Difford composed the music and Tilbrook wrote the lyrics.

Throughout the long period of Squeeze's musical successes, there was a rotation of musicians over the years, and although performing and touring all around the world, the band's two founder members, Difford and Tilbrook, continued a link to their roots by recording albums at Tilbrook's studio, 45RPM, located in Charlton.

After Difford moved to Firle, East Sussex, Squeeze sponsored Difford's local club Lewis FC, when former Charlton defender Steve Brown was the club's manager, the name of the band displayed on the front of the Rooks (Lewis FC's) shirt.

Tilbrook continued living in his local area of Charlton, and when not on tour or recording, occasionally performs at venues throughout Greenwich, as well as turning up for impromptu jamming sessions in local pubs.

Blooming great Charlton!!!

BUSTER'S

Buster Edwards

Ronald 'Buster' Edwards

Although born in Lambeth, it's been suggested over the years that Buster Edwards was a Charlton fan, however, as he spent so much time on the run, and then nine years locked up behind bars for his part in the Great Train Robbery, it's doubtful there was too much free time to get along to The Valley.

On leaving school, Edwards began work in a sausage factory but soon fell into criminal ways by stealing meat to sell on the post-war black market, then, when called up for national service and enrolling in the RAF, he was apprehended stealing cigarettes.

A former boxer and nightclub owner, Edwards was portrayed by Genesis drummer and vocalist Phil Collins in the film *Buster*, released in 1988, twenty-five years after the robbery when Edwards was thirty-two at the time of the heist.

In the romantic crime comedy-drama, The Addicks are mentioned twice, when Edwards supposedly went off to watch Charlton lose 4-0, and later, when Edwards is on the run and evading arrest living in Acapulco, he reads in an English Sunday newspaper Charlton had won at Manchester City, Eddie Firmani scoring twice.

After early release from prison, serving nine of a fifteen-year sentence for his part in the robbery, Edwards ran a flower stall outside Waterloo Station, but in a magazine interview he admitted, although he was going straight, life had become so dreary after his days of crime.

There has been continuing debate as to whether it was Edwards or Ronald Biggs, another Great Train robber, who was an actual Charlton fan, or even if neither were.

In the biography of footballer Stanley Mathews, he mentions meeting Biggs while on tour in Brazil, Biggs asking him how Charlton were doing and that he'd seen Mathews play at The Valley. It's also been suggested that a Charlton scarf was hung over the coffin of Biggs at his funeral. However, it's believed Biggs was really an Arsenal fan, as for Edwards, he's no longer around to ask, so the jury is still out.

Michael Grade

Son of entertainment agent and impresario Leslie Grade, and nephew of Lew Grade and Bernard Delfont, young Michael Grade had grown up in the world of showbiz and became a supporter of The Addicks through his family's association with the club. Educated at Stowe School Buckinghamshire and St Dunstan's College in London, Grade joined the Daily Mirror as a sports columnist in 1960, before moving into the theatrical business to take over from his father who suffered a stroke. Grade's career flourished when entering the television industry, joining London Weekend Television and then the USA-based Embassy TV.

When Charlton were about to leave The Valley for Selhurst Park, Grade also relocated to become Controller of the BBC, and often journeyed to South Norwood for Charlton matches, visiting the fish shop near the Sainsbury's end of the ground before kick-off, possibly dining on 'addick n chips!'

A fervent supporter of The Back to The Valley campaign and Valley Party, Grade joined Charlton's board of directors. After the club's return to The Valley, Grade was the main presenter of the Charlton Athletic Centenary History, a visual production charting the rise of The Addicks from a junior boys team playing on a piece of waste ground through to when the club were playing at a rebuilt Valley in the Premier League, plus all the highs and lows in between, of which there's been many.

Awarded a CBE in 1998 for services to broadcasting, Grade had coveted the role of chairman of the BBC board of governors, and when appointed in 2004, it was on the proviso that he wouldn't have to give up his Charlton directorship. During an interview, Grade was asked, what is your greatest fear? he replied, "Charlton Athletic getting relegated."

After a number of senior executive roles in television, Grade was created a life peer as Baron Grade of Yarmouth, Isle of White, and has been a member of the House of Lords since 2011.

UP THE Charlton!!!

Titter ye not!!!

Frankie Howerd

When Roger Alwen made the announcement Charlton intended to move back home to The Valley, after several seasons playing at Selhurst Park, up stepped Frankie Howerd to perform at the top of the bill in a benefit show at the Orchard Theatre, Dartford, in May 1989, the first event in a series of fundraising activities for the club.

Although born in York, Howerd's parents moved to southeast London where his father, a sergeant major, served in the army. Brought up in Eltham, Howerd attended Gordon Elementary School, where he first fell in love with show business when on a Boxing Day trip to a pantomime, *Cinderella*, at Woolwich Artillery Theatre.

Winning a scholarship at Woolwich County School, later Shooters Hill Grammar School, Howerd was praised for his theatrical skills and at the age of thirteen made his first appearance on stage. However, after failing an audition at RADA his intention of fulfilling a career in entertainment was put on hold, and Howerd began working as a filing clerk while continuing to tread the boards during his spare time.

Serving in the army as a bombardier during the latter part of the Second World War, Howerd also entertained the troops leading up to the D-Day landings, and was then promoted to sergeant before his unit sailed for the beaches of Normandy.

After being de-mobbed, Howerd began touring in the show, *For the Fun of it*, and soon found his way onto BBC Radio, with several other ex-service entertainers. From that time onwards, Howerd achieved his show business ambition, performing in radio, stage, film, and television productions, including appearances in *Carry-On* films, Shakespearean comedy roles, and the hugely popular TV comedy series *Up Pompeii*.

When the call came out from the organiser of Charlton's benefit night, Commercial Manager Steve Sutherland, Howerd didn't hesitate in offering his services, visiting the club's Sparrows Lane training ground for some publicity photographs before the show, and spending time talking with players and staff.

Karl Howman

An Addicks fan since a boy, Plumsted-born Karl Howman trained as a goalkeeper at Charlton when eleven, however, when he stopped growing after reaching the height of five-foot-eight, he moved on to his second passion acting, joining the National Youth Theatre.

Appearing in various stage, film, and television roles, Howman came to prominence after appearing in the television situation comedy, *Get Some In*, taking over the role of Jakey Smith from Robert Lindsey.

Best known for his starring role as the lovable painter and decorator Jacko in another popular sitcom *Brushstrokes*, Howman often mentioned the club and supporting Charlton as part of the dialogue during the series, which ran from 1986 to 1991. The length of the series corresponded with Charlton's run in the First Division, the top tier of the English Football League, while under the management of Lennie Lawrence.

In 1999, Howman made an appearance on Sky's Soccer AM, where he represented Charlton alongside his friend and working colleague Ray Winston, a West Ham fan.

When not on stage, filming or directing, Howman was often at The Valley on matchdays, and like most celebrity fans, after starting out standing with his mates on the terraces when young, as time moved on relocated to seats in the West Stand.

Occasionally turning out to play in charity matches for Charlton's Veterans teams, Howman also supported various club events and community projects which included the foundation of Valley Gold, before being appointed as a director of The South of England Foundation in connection with the work carried out by the Charlton Athletic Community Trust.

Although a lifelong Charlton fan, while residing in Kent, Howman was often spotted attending Ebbsfleet Town, matches, a club where various members of Charlton's managerial and playing staff moved on to after the Premier League years.

Now this is satisfaction!!!

Mick Jagger

When the Rolling Stones had their first ever number-one hit single cover, *It's All Over Now*, released in June 1964, Charlton were preparing for another season in the Second Division under manager Frank Hill, and many years had passed by since Mick Jagger and his brother Chris were taken to The Valley for the first time by their father Joe.

It was a time when The Addicks were still playing in the First Division, and legendary keeper Sam Bartram became Jagger's favourite player.

Born and raised in Dartford, Jagger, at the age of fourteen, appeared with his father, a physical education teacher, and former gymnast, on the ATV television series, *Seeing Sport*, promoting activities such as riding, swimming, athletics, judo, and Jagger's favourite sports, football, and cricket.

Educated at Wentworth Primary School, Dartford, where Jagger met future Rolling Stones band member Keith Richards, after passing his eleven-plus Jagger attended Dartford Grammar, and then the London School of Economics, however, he soon left education behind to form his own band.

After playing at local pubs and clubs for hardly any money at all, the Rolling Stones eventual recording success took them all around the world playing at sell-out concerts, which left little time for Jagger to attend his favourite sports in person.

Moving towards senior citizen age, Jagger dedicates a certain amount of his free time to attend Kent County Cricket matches at the St Lawrence Ground, Canterbury, where he could meet up with Kent's president and friend, former Charlton player and Kent County cricketer, Derek Ufton. On many occasions, Jagger and Ufton would discuss cricket and football over dinner and a few drinks.

Because of his love for cricket, Jagger launched a cricket website so he could check on scores while on tour, and after the final performance of the Rolling Stones world tour in 1998, invited guests and the press were flown to Istanbul for what was expected to be a wild celebration end of the concert party, however, as one of the press reported, Jagger wanted nothing more than to chat about Charlton.

Tutte Lemkow

One of the Addick's more obscure fans, Tutte Lemkow, a Norwegian-born television and film actor, dancer, singer, and guitarist, once had a trial to play football for Charlton, and although unsuccessful, went on to become an Addicks fan, or so the story goes.

Lemkow had moved to England with his first wife to pursue a career in ballet but went on to become an actor, playing mostly villainous or eccentric roles in television and film, appearing in productions such as *Moulin Rouge*, *Ben-Hur*, *Guns of Navarone*, *The Wrong Box*, *Indiana Jones*, and *Red Sonia*. The would-be footballer's television credits include *William Tell*, *The Avengers*, *Upstairs Downstairs*, *Jason King*, *UFO*, and *Doctor Who*.

Lemkow's most recognisable role came in the 1971 hit adaptation of the stage musical *Fiddler on the Roof*, playing a symbolic character, a fiddler, appearing intermittently throughout the film passionately playing his fiddle while dancing upon the roof of a timber-built house.

The author of Lemkow's obituary, published in the Sunday Times after the actor died in London early in November 1991, was unaware how Lemkow came to be offered a trial at Charlton, but it was suggested it may have been through the actor's various connections in the entertainment industry, a period when theatre and TV agents Lew and Leslie Grade were friends of Charlton's owners, the Gliksten brothers.

There seems to be no mention of Lemkow swapping his dancing shoes for football boots in the club's records, although not all the names of prospective trialists who didn't make the grade would have then been listed.

Whether the fiddler on the roof ever did have a trial for The Addicks, or indeed could knock a football about with as much skill as his dancing, may never be known, but the trial for Charlton was apparently Lemkow's own quoted anecdote, believe it or not.

Jonathan Maitland

Journalist, author, playwright, and broadcaster Jonathan Maitland, when on air during radio programmes, has professed his support of The Addicks, and often mentions the club during interviews and sports productions in which he appears. Growing up in Surrey, after attending Epsom College, and then graduating from King's College with a law degree, Maitland began his professional career writing for local newspapers.

Author of several books, Maitland was a general correspondent with the BBC before joining ITV presenting current affairs programmes and reporting on human interest stories, music, and sport. Residing in West London, Maitland played bass in a covers band, Surf 'n Turf, the group making it through to the final stages of a competition to find Britain's entry for the Eurovision Song Contest in 2002.

Maitland contributed and presented his own show and a variety of programmes for Five Live including *Up All Night*, discussing various topics, including Charlton.

A Nationally rated Scrabble player, Maitland runs his own cricket club, Riverbank Ramblers, which he founded in 1989, and as part of a media project, where Maitland attempted to make a million pounds over a year out of trading shares, the journalist invested £2,500 in Charlton when the club were heading for promotion as Champions to the Premier League in 2000, and why not?

Maitland was the subject of social media hacking during his investigative television programme into the pros and cons of the social media site, Facebook. As a test case, an investigating reporter, an expert in online technology safety and security, managed to hack into Maitland's own Facebook account, without his knowledge, after discovering through a news story, Maitland was a devoted Charlton supporter, gaining entry by using the password 'Charlton', which presumably Maitland has now changed.

How many other football fans use the name of the club they support as their password?

John Motson

Taken to his first-ever league game at The Valley by his father Reverend William Motson, Charlton drawing with Chelsea 1-1 at the end of the 1951-1952 season, the excitement of attending that game inspired a young John Motson to make scrapbooks of footballing facts. Motson also started collecting matchday programmes, which included Charlton's 1946 and 1947 FA Cup Finals.

Motson had previously been taken to watch Charlton reserve matches at The Valley when his family were living close to Plumstead Common, Motson usually taking up position either behind the North End goal or sitting in the old West Stand.

Born in Lancashire and educated in Suffolk, the family often moving around the country through his father's ministerial placements, Motson's professional career began as a newspaper reporter before joining the BBC as a sports presenter on Radio 2. Moving over to BBC TV, Motson became a regular commentator on *Match of the Day*, not only entertaining the viewers with his match commentaries but also with his various football facts and stats. Covering several Charlton matches at The Valley during the 1970s and early 1980s, as well as at Selhurst Park, although always remaining professionally impartial while on air, Motson has admitted he always had a soft spot for The Addicks.

Famous for his sheepskin coat, which Motson wore when covering matches during the height of the winter, when commentating at The Valley Motson had to climb up a precariously positioned ladder to access an open-to-the-elements commentary box, built from scaffold poles and wooden planks, erected high up on the old East Terrace.

When Charlton's director Roger Alwen announced the club's return to The Valley, after spending almost four seasons playing at Selhurst Park, a share scheme was issued to help raise funds for the club, and Motson was one of the first to apply, buying five-hundred shares.

Motson's best-remembered match, when commentating at The Valley, was Charlton's 4-0 win over Manchester City in August 2000. Before his retirement, Motson was often invited to speak at Charlton functions and supporter club meetings, which he was always more than willing to do.

Norman Pace

Well known as half of the comedy double act, Hale and Pace, Norman Pace met his future comedy partner Gareth Hale at Avery Hill Teacher Training College when student teachers, both intending to work in education.

Born in Dudley, Worcestershire, after moving to southeast London to attend college, Pace discovered a talent for comedy, and teaming up with Hale, they performed their comedy cabaret routine in local venues while continuing teacher training. Making his home in Kent, after qualifying as a teacher Pace worked in education for five years, an excellent source of comedy, before he and his teaching friend Hale, moved from education into comedy full time, the duo, going by the title Hale and Pace. Performing at local comedy venues, which included the Tramshed at Woolwich, Hale and Pace developed and honed their comedy act, ready for future television appearances, and expanded their stage material in the creation of a pair of straight-faced nightclub bouncers, The Two Rons.

Along with the Tramshed comedy group, Hale and Pace took to the stage in support of Charlton's Back to The Valley fundraising campaign at the Orchard Theatre Dartford, where Frankie Howerd topped the bill.

It seems it was Pace, rather than Hale, who caught The Addicks bug, and after the club directors secured the Sparrows Lane training ground as the first phase of Charlton's return home, he was invited to take part in the third annual training ground open day and launch of Valley Gold in August 1989. Pace joined in with other stars of entertainment and sport, including Karl Howman, Frazer Hines, Colin Cowdrey, Derek Underwood, and Alan Knott, to name just a few, playing football and cricket, and generally having a good laugh on the day.

A regular at The Valley during the club's Premier League years, after performing alongside his comedy act partner on stage, radio, and screen for over thirty years, in their own shows as well as making appearances in *The Young Ones*, *Doctor Who*, *Benidorm* and *Extras*, Pace then forged a successful solo career performing in the theatre, staring in *Chicago*, *Our Man in Havana*, *Annie Get Your Gun*, *The Rocky Horror Show* and *Hairspray*.

I'm a baking Addick !!!

Sue Perkins

Around the time the club relocated to Selhurst Park, Croydon-born comedian and presenter Sue Perkins was taken to Charlton matches for the first time by her father, an Addicks supporter and season ticket holder who lived close to The Valley, so as Perkins has admitted, there was no other choice.

Educated at Croham Hurst School Croydon, Perkins later studied English at the University of Cambridge, becoming a member of Footlights, an amateur dramatic club run by the students, where Perkins met her future creative comedy partner, Mel Giedroyc.

Under the title, Mel and Sue, the pair began their working relationship in television, writing and performing comedy, and co-hosting daytime chat shows. Perkins would go on to present various television productions, including *The Great British Bake Off*, joined once more by Giedroyc. The cookery competition series ran for seven seasons co-hosted by Perkins and Giedroyc.

Perkins also performed a solo comedy stand-up act at the Edinburgh Festival and regularly appears on a variety of light-entertainment shows and radio broadcasts.

A keen sports fan, keeping fit by taking up boxing, Perkins also loves football, usually watching rather than playing, and when at either of her homes, one in London and another in Cornwall, enjoys tuning in to a match broadcast on the TV.

When there was speculation over which football team the *Bake Off* presenter followed, Perkins, recognised for her quick wit and dry sense of humour, wrote on her Twitter account, "For those asking whether I'm a Gooner, know this. I support Charlton Athletic - the spiritual home of disappointment."

No doubt there are many Charlton fans who have felt much the same as Perkins has over the years.

Steve Rider

As most older supporters will know, when Charlton were playing in the 1998 Championship Play-Off Final on their way to the Premiership, Addicks fan Steve Rider had a TV monitor set up in the studio so he could watch the match broadcast live on Sky, while he was presenting Grandstand live for the BBC.

Born in Dartford and brought up not far from The Valley, Rider first began going to Charlton matches in 1959, and regularly attended games during the 1960s to 1970s, through the highs and lows of lower league football, before his career in sports journalism and broadcasting took him away, and up to another level.

Educated at John Roan Boys' Grammar School, Greenwich, Rider began his career working as a reporter for a local newspaper, before an opportunity came along to move into radio and television as a sports presenter. Relocating to Suffolk, Rider hosted Anglia TV's *Match of the Week*, where the only chance of watching Charlton was if they ever played a local club, which wasn't that often.

Leaving regional broadcasting behind, Rider first joined ITV's *World of Sport*, and then, leading up to Charlton's promotion from the Second Division to the First Division in 1986, Rider moved on to work as a presenter for the BBC, where he could then watch Addicks highlights on *Match of the Day*.

When Charlton finally made it up into the Premiership, Charlton's Supporters' Club consisted of several branches throughout the southeast, and although no longer living in the area, while attending a supporters' meeting as the special guest, Rider accepted an invitation to become president of the North West Kent Addicks branch.

Rider also turned out for the Charlton Quiz Team, alongside CEO Peter Varney, commercial manager Steve Sutherland, VOV editor Rick Everitt and club statistician Colin Cameron, winning the quiz competition.

Lee Ryan

Singer, songwriter, and actor, Lee Ryan, a member of the boy band Blue, has been an Addicks fan for many years, mentioning he followed the club on the band's official website.

A member of Blue since the band formed in 2000, Ryan was born in Chatham, and after attending school in

Belvedere, enrolled in a succession of performing art schools before joining Blue at the age of just sixteen.

Although Blue broke up in 2005, the members of the band no longer boys, they reformed as young men in 2009, and while not performing with Blue, Ryan also pursued a solo career. Releasing several singles and albums, and performing in various acting roles, Ryan was cast as bad boy heartthrob Harry 'Woody' Woodward in BBC's *EastEnders*. As a Charlton fan Ryan was most likely used to the seasonal pantomimes surrounding Charlton after the club's fall down the league divisions, and joined the cast of a panto himself when taking on the role of Aladdin, opposite Paul Merton's Widow Twanky......oh yes he did.

Appearing in two reality TV shows, *Hell's Kitchen* and *Celebrity Big Brother*, Ryan was also a contestant in *Strictly Come Dancing*, but went out in the third round, much like a majority of Charlton's cup exits.

Turning out to show off his football skills at charity matches, Ryan played at The Valley in the Annual Soccer Six fundraising football tournament, won by the X-Factor team, which included Ryan.

Often reported more recently in the media for his fiery temperament rather than for his musical and acting abilities, Ryan spends much of his time jetting off to various destinations around the globe. While on tour, as well as living abroad, Ryan still kept tabs on Charlton's results, and after becoming a father, which meant he was spending more time with his son in the UK, he's now converted him from a Gooner to an Addick.

John Sullivan

Although the writer of Only Fools and Horses was a devoted Arsenal fan, the first time Balham-born John Sullivan went to a football match was at The Valley, at around six years of age, taken to the game by his uncle Charlie, a Charlton supporter living in Bermondsey. Sullivan's memory of that day was the ground was the biggest place he had ever been.

During the time Sullivan attended matches at The Valley his favourite Charlton player was forward Lennie Glover.

When Sullivan was still a young boy his uncle Charlie passed away, and as the rest of his family were all Millwall fans, and he no longer had someone to take him, he stopped going.

After leaving school without any qualifications, Sullivan got his first job as a messenger boy and began attending Evening School classes studying German and English.

Submitting scripts to the BBC, Sullivan was employed in the props department, however, urged to continue writing by veteran comedy entertainer Ronnie Barker, he began to write scripts for the comedy sketch show *The Two Ronnies*, as well as comedian Dave Allen. Sullivan's big break came when a submitted script, *Citizen Smith*, was commissioned for BBC's *Comedy Special* in 1977, the pilot was so successful *Citizen Smith* was made into a series.

When an idea for a football comedy was rejected, Sullivan proposed an alternative based around a family of working-class market traders, and *Only Fools and Horses* was born, much of Sullivan's material based on his own life experiences living in south London.

Since the subjects of the series, the Trotter clan, came from southeast London it was natural they would support local football clubs, and during the series, there is mention of Del-Boy's father being a Millwall fan, and Del-Boy himself a Chelsea fan, up until they sold Jimmy Greaves. However, the best of all is when it's revealed Rodney's middle name was Charlton, given to him by his mother who was an Addicks fan.

Because his favourite uncle supported Charlton, Sullivan had warm memories of his days watching The Addicks, and always looked for their results, hoping they were doing well.

Keeping the beat with the Covered End Choir!!!

Steve and Alan White

Drumming brothers Steve and Alan White, from southeast London, have both been Addicks fans since young boys. Older brother Steve was taken to watch his first game, Charlton versus Bolton, by his grandfather in the 1970s, Alan, seven years younger, following in his brother's footsteps, much like their future musical career.

Given a drum by his uncle, Steve joined the Boys' Brigade so he could play in the band, and from then onwards, the drummer never looked back. Learning his trade through drumming lessons and listening to jazz records, then gigging with local bands, Steve became a major influence on his brother Alan, who also took up drumming.

Steve made his first drumming appearance at The Valley, aged only thirteen, his big break coming four years later when auditioning for a new band, Paul Weller's Style Council. As for Alan, at the age of fifteen, his first drumming audition was for the band Whirlpool, and although he didn't get the job, it wouldn't be too long before he was playing for another of the world's most successful bands.

Steve and Weller became great friends, and it was Weller who recommended Alan to Noel Gallagher when he was searching for a new drummer to join Oasis.

During The Addicks Premier League Years, Alan and Liam Gallagher were at The Valley when Charlton were up against Manchester City, both rival fans making a presentation on the pitch. Alan also took Red Hot Chili Peppers drummer Chad Smith to a match at The Valley, and Smith often asks the former Oasis drummer how the 'Reds' are doing.

When the Covered End choir's drummer needed a new drum, it was Steve who donated one of his own drums, part of a drum kit used when playing with Style Council.

The White family are all Charlton supporters and Steve and Alan's cousin Sarah played for the Charlton Women's team.

Epilogue

No doubt there will be even more Addicks celebrity fans to come, perhaps a few will be watching Charlton matches from the stands today, awaiting their chance to break into the world of arts and entertainment, whether it be in the music business, television and radio presenting and production, or treading the boards on stage and performing in television and film.

Perhaps, one day, there may be a celebrity Addicks fan out there who might just have the passion, as well as enough spare cash in the bank earning interest, who'll take a risk of buying the club, before the curtain comes down on another unproductive seasonal run, and direct Charlton back on the road to a successful revival.

Printed in Great Britain
by Amazon

45466488R00046